Praxeology and Understanding: An Analysis of the Controversy in Austrian Economics

by George A. Selgin

The Ludwig von Mises Institute
Auburn University
Auburn, Alabama 36849

Copyright © 1990 The Ludwig von Mises Institute

All rights reserved. Written permission must be secured from the publisher to use or reproduce any part of this book, except for brief quotations in critical reviews or articles.

Published by Praxeology Press of the Ludwig von Mises Institute, Auburn University, Auburn, Alabama 36849

Library of Congress Catalog Card Number: 90-062373
ISBN: 0-945466-09-9

Contents

Preface	5
Praxeology and Understanding	9
Praxeology: The Method of Economic Theory	11
Ideal Types and "Exact Laws"	18
From Mises to Lachmann: Austrian Revisionism	27

    Hayek • Shackle • Lachmann

Equilibration and Coordination	37

    Equilibration • Kirzner, Lachmann, and the "Tendency toward Equilibrium" • Prerequisites for Successful Action • The "Common Sense" of Coordination

The Implications of the "Kaleidic Society"	59
References	69
About the Author	73
About the Ludwig von Mises Institute	74

Preface

The essay reprinted here is from the 1987 *Review of Austrian Economics* and is based upon a longer one written in 1982, when I was a second-year graduate student at New York University. That essay was composed in response to a seemingly indeterminable debate among participants in the N.Y.U. Austrian economics colloquium. The debate centered around the question of whether any "tendency toward equilibrium" is present in market economies. Israel Kirzner believed wholeheartedly in the tendency; Ludwig Lachmann was equally firm in his skepticism. The graduate students were more or less equally divided on the issue.

The obvious lack of progress in this controversy had convinced me that the disagreements involved resided in matters of definition or (a more troubling possibility) in some fundamental schism. Thinking furthermore that Ludwig von Mises's own epistemological views were being inadequately appreciated on both sides of the debate, I decided to get involved. Part of my contribution was to suggest an alternative notion of "equilibration," based upon a more consistent application of methodological subjectivism. My approach was, I think, consistent with prior developments in value theory which had stripped concepts like value, cost, and utility of their "objective" connotations, recasting them as purely subjective (or, in earlier parlance, "psychological") magnitudes. A like revision of the concepts of rent and profit was, in my opinion, long overdue. The latter revision of the concepts led quite naturally to a new and strictly logical ("praxeological") view of the equilibrative process—a view which could withstand the onslaught of Shacklian nihilism. Thus Kirzner (and, I think, Mises also) were to be saved by means of a consistent application of Lachmannian radical subjectivism! I confidently and naïvely expected to win converts on both sides.

In the event my confidence was displaced: rather than resolve the controversy I merely succeeded in creating another division. Both Kirzner and Lachmann were unmoved. Even worse was the response of several graduate students who argued that my efforts were nothing more than an exercise in argument by authority. Having observed my frequent use of quotations by Mises, they apparently lost track of the fact that the paper was, after all, largely intended as an interpretation and defense of Mises's views. At George Mason University the paper provoked a similar, negative response.

All told, my critics appeared to me to have placed a disproportionate emphasis upon the lack of originality of what I had written. This was matched by a corresponding lack of attention to the arguments themselves. There may have been serious flaws in my logic; yet my harshest critics were unable or unwilling to point the flaws out to me.

A few bouquets did manage to float their way along the stream of criticisms against my essay. Murray Rothbard was an early source of encouragement: I still recall with great pleasure the evening spent with him in his New York apartment as he painstakingly reviewed my first draft. Far more unexpected were the kind remarks of G.L.S. Shackle, of all people, who saw some virtue in my arguments despite the fact that they were largely directed against him. Finally there was a lengthy and constructive report by a referee for *Economics and Philosophy*, who also detected the hand of Mises in what I had to say but viewed this as a mark in my essay's favor. Thus it appeared that, to more "mainstream" theorists and also to non-Austrian outsiders like Shackle, "Misesian" thinking had its merits; whereas for many self-styled "Austrians" Misesian arguments had become strictly taboo!

That trend appears, fortunately, to have ended, and the adjective "Misesian" no longer serves (among the majority of Austrians, at least) as a term of opprobrium. The way is therefore clear for a more constructive reconsideration of "Praxeology and Understanding" against the background of recent debates within the Austrian school. Such circumstances make it a special delight for me to see "Praxeology and Understanding: An Analysis of the Controversy in Austrian Economics" reprinted. For this and other kindnesses extended to me in recent years by the Ludwig von Mises Institute, I am grateful.

George Selgin
Athens, Georgia
July, 1990

Praxeology and Understanding: An Analysis of the Controversy in Austrian Economics

George A. Selgin

The law of sufficient reason states the minimum amount of connection and order in the world which is necessary if we are to have a chance to understand and control it.... Thus [the law asserts] there is not unlimited possibility present in our world.... Whatever occurs, a battle, a change in the government or in the economic system, or the like, it is not true that everything or anything else could have happened...

The principle of sufficient reason obviously cannot be proved objectively; that is, we cannot prove that it was impossible for everything which has happened to have been different, and we certainly cannot prove that the present constitution of the world is such that only certain things will happen and that nothing else can possibly occur. It is rather a postulate of science to satisfy the demand for understanding.... By assuming, therefore, that everything has certain determinate relations to certain definite other elements we have a reason for seeking to find them, and the success of science or its progress encourages us to believe that further relations can be discovered if we persist in our search.

—Morris Cohen
The Meaning of Human History, pp. 97, 100

> We live in a world full of contradiction and paradox, a fact of which perhaps the most fundamental illustration is this: that the existence of a problem of knowledge depends on the future being different from the past, while the possibility of the solution of the problem depends on the future being like the past.
>
> —Frank Knight
> *Risk, Uncertainty and Profit*, p. 313

Austrian economics emerged in rebellion against skepticism. The predominant economic doctrine in continental Europe at the time of its founding, that championed by the German historical school under Gustav Schmoller, rejected the idea of an economic science devoted to the explanation of market phenomena in terms of exact and universal laws. It proposed, instead, historical description and interpretation of social events devoid of any reference to universal or "exact" laws and to "pure" economic theories based on them.

Today, Austrian economics is challenged by skepticism once again. The new threat is not historicism per se, but the unorthodox views of G. L. S. Shackle and his Austrian followers.[1] According to Shackle, the future is unknowable and "kaleidic" (that is, dominated by patternless change). Action in the marketplace, to be rational, requires that actors in the marketplace be able to anticipate the behavior of their fellows. Theory cannot explain why such anticipations should, except by mere chance, be correct. Thus the idea that action is "purposeful," which lies at the heart of the conventional Austrian

---

[1] For evidence of Shackle's influence, see *Method, Process, and Austrian Economics*, Israel M. Kirzner, ed. (Lexington, Mass.: Lexington Books, 1982).

approach to economic theory, is questioned, and new doubt is cast upon the meaningfulness of economic science. This has led to a controversy within the Austrian school that is the subject of the present analysis.

Before examining this controversy, it will be necessary to review the methodological tenets of Austrian economics. In particular, it will be useful to examine the method of praxeology, which forms the basis for the Austrian defense of the possibility and validity of "pure" (i.e., universal) economic theory. The investigation will then proceed to analyze the ideas of F. A. Hayek, G. L. S. Shackle, and Ludwig M. Lachmann insofar as they have cast suspicion upon the praxeological approach as it was originally conceived by Ludwig von Mises. Finally, the analysis will turn to the issues of equilibration, coordination, and determinism that occupy center stage in current Austrian debate. It attempts to resolve the conflicts concerning these issues by offering new arguments based on the application of radical subjectivism consistent with the praxeological framework. The article concludes with a critical assessment of proposed changes in the Austrian "research program."

Praxeology: The Method of Economic Theory

The most conscientious and extensive development of the methodological doctrines of the Austrian school was undertaken by Ludwig von Mises.[2] Mises viewed his

---

[2]See the following by Mises, *Human Action*, 3rd ed. (Chicago: Henry Regnery, 1966), chaps. 1-4; *Epistemological Problems of Economics* (New York: New York University Press, 1981); *Theory and History* (New Haven: Yale University Press, 1957); and *The Ultimate Foundation of Economic Science* (Kansas City, Kans.: Sheed Andrews and McMeel, 1978).

efforts as an elaboration and extension of the beliefs of Carl Menger, the school's founder. Menger's views developed during the course of the famous *Methodenstreit*, which pitted him against the antitheoretical doctrines of the German historical school. Lachmann aptly notes that Mises "saw in Menger's distinction between 'exact laws' and empirical regularities the pivot of Austrian methodology."[3] Mises's particular elaboration of the Austrian method, which he called "praxeology,"[4] is still regarded by many Austrian economists as *the* method of the Austrian school.[5]

In refining Menger's ideas, Mises had to confront new opposition in the form of the doctrines of logical positivism. Mises saw in positivism the same epistemological presumptions that were at work in historicism; namely, a denial of the existence of universal and necessary laws independent of concrete historical events. To Mises this view was grounded in fallacy:

> We are not capable of conceiving a world in which things would not run their course "according to eternal, pitiless, grand laws." But this much is clear to us. In a world so constituted, human thought and "rational" human action would not be possible. And therefore in such a world there could be neither human beings nor logical thought.[6]

---

[3]Ludwig M. Lachmann, "Ludwig von Mises and the Extension of Subjectivism," in Kirzner, *Method, Process, and Austrian Economics*, p. 32.

[4]Professor Lachmann also refers to his own method as praxeology. In this study, the term *praxeology* is used in the narrower sense employed by Mises and Rothbard as well as by Kirzner in *The Economic Point of View* (Kansas City, Kans.: Sheed and Ward, 1976).

[5]Cf. Murray N. Rothbard, "Praxeology: The Method of Austrian Economics," in *The Foundations of Modern Austrian Economics*, Edwin G. Dolan, ed. (Kansas City, Kans.: Sheed Andrews and McMeel, 1976), pp. 19-39.

[6]Mises, *Epistemological Problems of Economics,* pp. 197-98.

Empiricism, beginning with Hume's skepticism and including all of its positivist variants, shares the historicist's denial of necessity. It attempts to salvage the categories of "law" and "theory" by invoking the procedure of induction, i.e., the derivation of theory from the generalization of observed conjunctions of historical events. However, empiricism has yet to solve the "problem of induction." It cannot, on the basis of its own epistemological tenets, offer a satisfactory basis for the assumption that its generalizations apply with equal force to *future* events.[7] Thus empiricism does not provide a true alternative to historicism. It leaves intact the claim, disputed by Menger and by Mises, that scientific knowledge consists entirely of generalizations "drawn from past experience that could always be upset by some later experience."[8]

In countering positivism Mises took refuge in Kantian epistemology and especially in Kant's defense of the category of the synthetic a priori. What Mises regarded as crucial in Kant was, however, not Kant's formal analysis of a priori knowledge or his epistemological idealism, but rather his conviction, *contra* empiricism and historicism, that reason could give universal and necessary knowledge—knowledge that was fresh and informative.[9] In the sense in which he applied it in economics, Mises's apriorism did not differ fundamentally from Menger's Aristotelian essentialism.[10]

---

[7]On empiricism and the "problem of induction," see Errol Harris, *Hypothesis and Perception* (London: George Allen & Unwin, 1970), chaps. 1-4. Cf. also David Hume's *Treatise of Humane Nature*, bk. 1, pt. 3, sec. 6.

[8]Mises, *Epistemological Problems of Economics*, p. 5.

[9]See Brand Blanshard, *Reason and Analysis* (La Salle, Ill.: Open Court, 1973), p. 82.

[10]See Lawrence H. White, *The Methodology of the Austrian School of Economics* (Auburn, Ala.: Ludwig von Mises Institute, 1984), p. 7.

Praxeology represents an attempt to escape the nihilistic implications of both historicism and empiricism. It affirms the operation of inviolable laws within the realm of human action. It purports to establish the universal validity of these laws by deducing them from the allegedly incontestable truth that people act purposefully, the "axiom of action." Although supposedly irrefutable, this axiom is not merely "analytic," i.e., nonempirical or vacuous. It is based upon the reality of the pursuit of ends and the choice of means for their attainment that distinguishes all mental (and, hence, human) activity.[11] Thus *a priori* to Mises means "independent of any particular time or place." It does not imply independence from all "experience," although it does denote independence from the sort of sensory experience that empiricism and positivism emphasize: "It rests on universal *inner* experience, and not simply on external experience, i.e., its evidence is reflective rather than physical."[12] Sense data alone, on the other hand, could not reveal to us the essential purposefulness of human actions.

Nor is experience of the empiricist variety effective in refuting theories derived praxeologically. Rather, refutation of a praxeological theory requires discovery of a fault in the chain of reasoning employed by the praxeologist. Empirical evidence does not "falsify" a theory, but rather serves to establish the appropriateness of the theory's application to a particular, concrete event.[13]

---

[11]William James, *The Principles of Psychology* (New York: Dover, 1950), p. 8.

[12]Murray N. Rothbard, "In Defense of 'Extreme Apriorism'," *Southern Economic Journal* 23, no. 3 (January 1957): 314-20.

[13]Mises, *Epistemological Problems of Economics*, p. 30.

To meaningfully deny the "action axiom" (i.e., the claim that people act purposefully) is difficult. Denial of the axiom's empirical validity involves a purposeful act on the part of skeptics. It therefore confronts them with the uncomfortable choice of either conceding the issue or proclaiming that their own disagreement is purposeless. Thus any denial of the action axiom is self-contradictory.[14] Yet it is neither "empty" nor "arbitrary": it is axiomatic in the sense that distinguishes an *axiom* from a *postulate*. It is epistemologically distinct from the a priori assumptions employed in the hypothetical-deductive procedures of orthodox (neoclassical) economics.[15]

To be sure, Mises would have insisted that all of the lasting discoveries of the classical and neoclassical economists in the realm of pure theory were in fact results of the method described by praxeology; but this was by no means the *acknowledged* procedure of those schools of thought.[16] Neoclassical economics regards even its most fundamental "laws" as contingent or "probable." Indeed, many of its modern theorems are based upon patently false assumptions, some selected for their alleged predictive capacity and all subject to empirical testing and falsification. The fundamental "laws" of praxeology are,

---

[14]See William P. Montague, *The Ways of Knowing* (London: George Allen & Unwin, 1925), p. 90: "The truth of a given proposition is proved to be necessary when its contradictory implies self-contradiction." As a general point, it should be noted that the positivist assertion that all a priori statements are either tautologous or meaningless is itself a priori and therefore, by their criteria, meaningless (since it is by no means a tautology). See Blanshard, *Reason and Analysis*, p. 240. The source of the argument from contradiction is Aristotle's *Metaphysics*, bk. 1, chap. 3.

[15]*Contra* John B. Egger. See "The Austrian Method," in *New Directions in Austrian Economics*, Louis M. Spadaro, ed. (Kansas City, Kans.: Sheed Andrews and McMeel, 1978), p. 20.

[16]But see Marion Bowley, *Nassau Senior and Classical Economics* (New York: Octagon Books, 1964), chap. 1, on Senior's anticipation of the praxeological method.

in contrast, held by it to be universally valid. They hold with "apodictic certainty."[17]

Mises was heavily influenced by Max Weber as well as by Kant. It was from Weber that Mises took the notion of purposefulness which he made the starting point of praxeological analysis. Mises also adopted Weber's emphasis upon methodological individualism and his insistence upon the necessity and possibility of an entirely value-free (*wertfrei*) science of human action.[18] Using these notions, Mises refined Menger's development of the subjective theory of value.

Mises's extended application of praxeological subjectivism may be viewed as a limited version of the doctrine of epistemological subjectivism or idealism: it maintains that within the realm of human action, there are phenomena—in particular, market phenomena—that exist only by virtue of the consciousness of purposeful individuals. Thus value, wealth, profit, loss, and costs are products of human thought, having no "objective" or extensive foundation. One cannot imagine their existence or conceive their alteration, except in connection with acts of

---

[17]Richard Langlois says, regarding the notion of "apodictic certainty," that "the post-Humean mind rebels at the hubris of such a claim" ("Austrian Economics as Affirmative Science: Comment on Rizzo" in Kirzner, *Method, Process, and Austrian Economics*, p. 82). According to defenders of praxeology, such "post-Humean" thinking is itself problematic. It involves a denial of necessity and causation that, taken seriously, would lead to the abandonment of all theoretical and historical pursuits. (Cf. Morris Cohen, *The Meaning of Human History* [La Salle, Ill.: Open Court, 1961], pp. 64, 101-02.) We shall see that the controversy in Austrian economics is a direct consequence of misguided attempts to apply such "post-Humean" thinking to the theoretical science of human action.

[18]See Weber's essay "'Objectivity' in Social Science and Social Policy," in *Methodology of the Social Sciences*, Edward Shils and H. A. Finch, ed. (Glencoe, Ill.: Free Press, 1949), pp. 49-112.

valuation and choice.[19] (I shall have occasion to insist upon the consistent application of this subjective doctrine later on.) Thus to explain market phenomena in a manner consistent with its subjectivism, praxeology refers to acts of valuation and choice. However, praxeological subjectivism is also value-free or nonnormative:

> [It] does not pass judgment on action, but takes it exactly as it is, and it explains market phenomena not on the basis of "right" action, but on the basis of given action. It does not seek to explain the exchange ratios that would exist on the assumption that men are governed exclusively by certain motives and that other motives do in fact govern them, have no effect. It wants to comprehend the formation of exchange ratios that actually appear in the market.[20]

Praxeology is also distinct from psychology. Although it explains market phenomena in terms of individual purposefulness, it does not seek to identify the motivations, thoughts, and ends that give rise to particular purposes and choices. The inability of the praxeologists, as "pure theorists," to identify the ends of acting individuals also prevents them from constructing categories of "economic" and "noneconomic" action. Moreover, it prohibits them from passing judgment on the appropriateness of individual choices. Because praxeology does not judge actions, it is also not in a position to regard any act as "irrational." It recognizes that all acts of choice have meaning to the individual choosers in terms of *some* goal or purpose, however peculiar or ephemeral, that directs their actions: "The idea of an

---

[19] We shall see how this view applies to the concepts of entreperneurial profit and equilibration in section "Equilibration and Coordination."

[20] Mises, *Epistemological Problems of Economics*, pp. 180-81.

action not in conformity with needs is absurd. As soon as one attempts to distinguish between the need and the action and makes the need the criterion for judging the action, one leaves the domain of theoretical science, with its neutrality in regard to value judgments."[21] This application of subjectivism freed praxeology from psychological or normative assumptions and made it the analysis of the "pure logic of choice." Through it economics could become a means for the discovery of universal truths. Subjectivism was not wanted for its own sake, but as a means toward the Austrian quest for elements of necessity within the sequence of social events.

Ideal Types and "Exact Laws"

Praxeological theories, as understood by Mises, are independent of the particular psychological makeup of individuals. Praxeology does not address the *content* of individual preferences or the particular motives that give rise to those preferences. It is concerned with the pure *logic* of choice.

Concrete individual ends and values have historical but not theoretical significance; that is, they are relevant to all applications of pure theory to particular, historical circumstances, but enter only as auxiliary assumptions in constructing theory itself. Individual ends and calculations undergo continuous inexplicable change and cannot be the subject of anything like "exact laws." In the words of Frank Knight, a non-Austrian defender of the

---

[21]Ibid., p. 149. See also Mises, "The Treatment of 'Irrationality' in the Social Sciences," *Philosophy and Phenomenological Research* 4, no. 4 (June 1944): 527-53, reprinted in *Money, Method, and the Market Process: Essays by Ludwig von Mises*, Richard Ebeling, ed. (Boston: Kluwer Academic Publishers, 1990), pp. 16-36.

praxeological method, "There are no laws regarding the *content* of economic behavior, but there are laws universally valid as to its *form*. There is an abstract rationale of all conduct which is rational at all, and a rationale of social relations arising through the organization of rational activity."[22]

To distinguish its universally valid content from history, praxeology had to show that its most fundamental theoretical conclusions—its theoretical "hard core"—was not based upon the imputation of some "typical" motivations or values to acting people. For this reason Mises, while adopting many of Max Weber's methodological prescriptions, regarded the latter's "ideal-type" constructs as unnecessary to the development of pure theory. For Mises, the laws of praxeology did not refer to ideal-type "rational" or "economic" people, but to acting people *as such*. Only in this way could those laws be universal or, in Menger's word, "exact."

Weber, in contrast, had been unable to accept Menger's notion of exact laws in economics. Thus he regarded the "law" of diminishing marginal utility and other fundamental discoveries of the pure logic of choice as "pragmatic" rather than necessary truths.[23] Weber considered economic theory dependent upon the assumption of special kinds of action that might in fact only loosely approximate the actions of people in the real world. In particular, Weber referred to a type of "rational man" who was a throwback to the "economic man" of the

---

[22]Frank Knight, "The Limitations of Scientific Method in Economics," in *The Ethics of Competition and Other Essays* (New York: Harper Bros., 1935), p. 25.

[23]See Ludwig Lachmann, *The Legacy of Max Weber* (Berkeley, Calif.: The Glendessary Press, 1971), p. 25.

classical economists.[24] Mises, in contrast, held that such an approach was, first of all "wholly inapplicable to the subjective value theory" and, further, that it failed "to solve the question of the source of this knowledge of 'purely economic' behavior."[25]

A more fundamental problem with the ideal-type approach is recognized by Israel Kirzner in his book *The Economic Point of View*. "It is apparent," Kirzner writes, "that when conformity to an ideal-type must be assumed for the deductions of the propositions of economics, these propositions cease to be logical implications of actions, and economics ceases to be a branch of praxeology."[26] In other words, economic laws become contingent rather than necessary, and the ideal-type approach fails to provide economic theory with an epistemological basis that frees it from the defects of positivism and historicism.

Alfred Schutz, in his 1932 book, *The Phenomenology of the Social World*, accepted Mises's criticisms of Weber

---

[24]Thus, in his *Methodology of the Social Sciences*, Weber writes:
> Pure economic theory . . . utilizes ideal-type concepts exclusively. [It] makes certain assumptions which scarcely ever correspond completely with reality but which approximate it in various degrees and asks: how would men act under these assumed conditions *if* their actions were entirely rational? It assumes the dominance of *pure economic interests* and precludes the operation of political or other non-economic considerations. (pp. 43-44; emphasis added)

Compare this to Mill's summary of the classical method: "Political economy . . . reasons from *assumed* premises—from premises which might be totally without foundation in fact, and which are not pretended to be universally in accordance with it" (John Stuart Mill, *Essays on Some Unsettled Questions of Political Economy*, 2nd ed. [London: Longmans, Green, Reader, and Dyer, 1874], p. 137).

[25]Ludwig von Mises, *Notes and Recollections* (South Holland, Ill.: Libertarian Press, 1978), p. 122. See also, *Epistemological Problems of Economics*, pp. 74-79.

[26]Israel Kirzner, *The Economic Point of View* (Menlo Park, Calif.: Institute for Humane Studies, 1976), p. 159.

and attempted to incorporate these into his own adaption and generalization of Weber's method.[27] Schutz proposed an ideal-type for acting man which would possess the universal applicability needed for the construction of pure economic theory. According to Schutz, ideal-types of this sort "do not refer to any individual or spatio-temporal collection of individuals. They are statements about anyone's action, about action or behavior considered as occurring in complete anonymity and without any specification of time or place. They are precisely for that reason lacking in concreteness."[28] Schutz observed, using words taken from Mises, that any principle derived from such constructs is "not a statement about what usually happens, but of what necessarily must happen."[29]

Schutz here stretches the meaning of ideal-type so as to include constructs so "typical" or general that no action can be conceived that does not conform to them. If we so define *ideal-type* to include a type of mankind "as such," then we may conclude that praxeological theories must also be based "exclusively" on the use of ideal-typical constructs.

The significance of Schutz's work to Austrian economics lies not in this semantic innovation but rather in Schutz's use of more *narrow* ideal-types to derive what he calls a "common sense" understanding of social phenomena. This common sense approach is, however, *not* based upon the anonymous ideal-type of mankind "as

---

[27]Alfred Schutz, *The Phenomenology of the Social World*, George Walsh and Frederick Lehnhart, trans. (1932; Evanston, Ill.: Northwestern University Press, 1967), pp. 242-45.

[28]Ibid., p. 244.

[29]Ibid., p. 245. Mises refers to Schutz's book in *Epistemological Problems of Economics* (pp. 125-26 f n.), but proposes to "reserve dealing with [Schutz's] ideas for another work." The promised discussion has never appeared in print.

such." It is, as is readily apparent from Schutz's own discussion of it, a historical, value-laden approach: "In order to explain human actions the scientist has to ask what *model* of an individual mind can be constructed and what typical *contents* must be attributed to it in order to explain *observed facts* as the results of the activity of such a mind in an understandable relation."[30] These models, Schutz continues, "are models of rational actions but not of actions performed by living human beings in situations defined by them."[31]

It is clear that Schutz is describing a procedure that Mises would have regarded as historical (i.e., suitable for examining particular, concrete cases) rather than praxeological. Mises's distinction between theory and history was a sharp one, and I shall have occasion to discuss it later. What must now be understood is that for Mises economic theory rests upon a body of certain truths independent of time and place. The presence of such a "pure" theoretical foundation distinguishes praxeology from types of economic analysis that regard even their most fundamental assertions as empirical, i.e., as "historically limited" in nature.

For Weber, in contrast (as Mises interpreted him):

> The difference between [praxeology] and history is considered as only one of degree. ... They are different merely in the extent of their proximity to reality, their fullness of content, and the purity of their ideal-typical construction. Thus Max Weber has implicitly answered the question that had once constituted the *Methodenstreit* [the famous Battle of Methods in which Carl Menger defended theoretical

---

[30]From the reprint in Maurice Natanson, *Philosophy of the Social Sciences* (New York: Random House, 1963), p. 342; emphasis added.

[31]Ibid., p. 345.

analysis against the attacks of the historical school] entirely in the sense of those who denied the logical legitimacy of a theoretical science of social phenomena. According to him [praxeology] is logically conceivable only as a special, qualified kind of historical investigation.[32]

In the analysis of history (which for Mises includes most "applied" economics), the use of content-laden ideal types is unavoidable: in order to render meaningful in other than a logical sense the particular acts of persons and the concrete consequences that arise from and in turn influence those acts, one needs to impute to the persons in question a framework of motivations, ends, and imagined means, thus making their behavior *understandable*. This method of historical understanding or *verstehen* (which is the same as Schutz's "common sense" approach to observed facts) goes beyond the logical, necessary aspects of action and attempts to reconstruct the psychological content and orientation of actions. It analyzes actions, not merely by referring to human purposefulness, but by attempting to comprehend the subjective *meaning* attached to actions by the actors themselves. As such, its constructs cannot refer only to the anonymous figure of acting man or man "as such," but instead must refer to preference-laden, idealized individuals.

For Mises, "history" deals with the *concrete* manifestations of action. "For history," he observed, "the main question is: What was the meaning the actors attached to the situation in which they found themselves and what was the meaning of their reaction and, finally, what was the *result* of these actions."[33] In an important sense,

---

[32]Mises, *Epistemological Problems of Economics*, p. 77.

[33]Mises, *The Ultimate Foundation of Economic Science*, p. 43; emphasis added.

then, the pure theory that forms the heart of praxeological analysis requires a type of subjectivism distinct from the subjectivism needed in historical analysis. Praxeologists, as developers of pure theory, must consider market phenomena without presuming any knowledge of agents' preferences and beliefs. They must view the world, not as "understanding" beings employing "common sense" to interpret a specific historical event, but as theorists in search of the *logical* patterns that underlie the actions of *all* "understanding" individuals.

Of course, even pure economic theory is affected to some degree by considerations of history. But these considerations mainly refer to the problem of whether a certain theory is relevant to a particular historical phenomenon under investigation. Thus the law of diminishing marginal utility and its immediate corollaries apply with certainty to any historical situation where at least one purposeful individual must dispose of (or sacrifice) multiple units of a good. The Ricardian law of association, in contrast, applies only where there are numerous individuals engaged in exchange, that is, it is a law pertaining to market phenomena, or what Hayek called "catallactics." Other praxeological laws and theories rely upon lengthier chains of reasoning into which a variety of assumptions enter. These are hypothetical-deductive theories: although their starting point is the certain fact of purposefulness, the auxiliary assumptions involved may or may not conform to any particular historical circumstances. Finally, praxeology includes exercises in "conjectural history" in which reference is made to specific institutions (money, central banking), circumstances (monopoly), and policies (tariffs, taxation). Such conjectural histories therefore make use of ideal-type constructs (these constructs, to be sure, never refer to ideal-typical *people*, but only to ideal-type *objects* or *consequences* of action), although their truth follows apodictically wherever all the real-life equivalents of the specified ideal-types are present in a given historical circumstance. Causal-genetic or "evolutionary" theories such as Menger's theory of the origin of money fall into this category of conjectural history.

Praxeologists may sometimes refer to *actual* historical events in order to *illustrate* theoretical results. Here, however, a casual exercise in history proper (and, therefore, a departure from pure theory) is involved. All examinations of particular historical policies and institutions—e.g., all "applied economics," which, to be sure, includes most of what economists do—are nevertheless outside the realm of pure theory and necessarily rely upon assumptions about individual motives and values. Thus actual history, unlike the conjectural histories of the praxeologist, makes use of ideal-type constructs, not only of institutions, policies, and industrial circumstances, but also of acting individuals. It seeks to understand the specific meaning of historical market phenomena by referring to "common sense" interpretations based upon values and goals imputed to the actors involved. The dividing line between "theory" (i.e., praxeology) and history (in Mises's strict sense) is thus marked by the need to employ psychological understanding or "common sense."

"Common sense," however, is not used only by social scientists. Praxeology recognizes it is an essential tool of all people who act in the social world. All entrepreneurial action (i.e., speculative action in the marketplace) requires understanding of other people's motives and intentions: "To know the future reactions of other people is the first task of acting man. Knowledge of their past value judgments and actions, although indispensable, is only a means to this end."[34] Thus, while history and common sense or psychological understanding of people's *past* values and actions are essential for understanding the future, they are not necessarily sufficient. Moreover, entrepreneurship derives only limited practical guidance from praxeology, the "predictions" of which, being simply examples of its conjectural histories, are always qualitative and contingent; they cannot inform us of the actual choices people will make. "The a priori discipline of human action, praxeology, does not deal with the actual content of value judgments. It deals only with the fact that men value and then act according to their valuations. What we know about the actual content of judgments of value can be derived only from experience."[35]

With these considerations in mind, it is possible to state the dilemma at the heart of the present controversy in Austrian economics: If, in fact, "action [in society] *implies* understanding of other men's reactions"[36] and "no action can be planned or executed without an understanding of the future,"[37] then how can praxeology proceed to the elucidation of market phenomena unless it *first* addresses "the main epistemological problem of ... understanding," *viz.*: "How can a man have any knowledge of the future value judgments and actions of other people?"[38] The current controversy within the Austrian school is due mainly to the conviction on the part of some Austrians that praxeology must address and resolve this

---

[34] Mises, *Theory and History*, p. 311.
[35] Ibid.
[36] Mises, *The Ultimate Foundation of Economic Science*, p. 49.
[37] Ibid., p. 50.
[38] Mises, *Theory and History*, p. 311.

problem of understanding. Otherwise, its theorems must be regarded, not as *necessary* truths about the world, but as empty and arbitrary tautologies referring to a hypothetical society populated, not necessarily by man "as such," but by "understanding man"; not by *homo agens*, but by *homo percipiens* (perceiving man) and, even more crucially, by *homo divinans*—"man who grasps the future."

From Mises to Lachmann: Austrian Revisionism

Hayek

A break from the praxeological approach came with Friedrich Hayek's 1937 essay "Economics and Knowledge."[39] The intention of this essay was ambiguous. Superficially, it appeared to be a critique of neoclassical equilibrium analysis. But it also involved a subtle rejection of the methodological presuppositions of praxeology.[40]

Though admitting that Austrian economics did possess a "formal" component (which Hayek called the "pure logic of choice"), Hayek regarded the meaningfulness and necessary truth of this formal component to be severely circumscribed. Indeed, he viewed praxeology as only contingently applicable to catallactics, i.e., to the eluci-

---

[39]Hayek's "Economics and Knowledge" was first published in *Economica* n.s. 4 (1937): 33-54, and reprinted with revisions in *Individualism and Economic Order* (Chicago: University of Chicago Press, 1948), pp. 33-56. All references are to the reprint.

[40]Hayek only recently made public his rejection of the praxeological method. (See "An Interview with F. A. Hayek," in Cato *Policy Report* 5 [February 1983]: 6-7). Nevertheless, he has long maintained that his intention in 1937 had been to show Mises the deficiencies in the praxeological approach.

dation of market phenomena. As far as the social world was concerned, the pure logic of choice was merely a collection of empirically empty tautologies.[41] Praxeology, in seeking "apodictically certain" conclusions, had so drained itself of content as to become useless as an *independent* means for deriving useful truths about reality. Far from relying exclusively upon the fact of purposefulness, applications of praxeology to catallactic phenomena involve unacknowledged auxiliary assumptions about the dissemination and use of *knowledge* by market participants; assumptions *"about causation in the real world."*[42] This is true especially of its conclusions that rely upon the operation of competitive forces with a "tendency toward equilibrium" as their driving force. And where assumptions about causation are involved, these are subject to falsification.[43]

Hayek's allusions to falsification are a special source of ambiguity, for one is never entirely sure whether the implied empirical analysis is supposed to make use of the crude sense of data of positivism or of "common sense" evaluation founded on ideal-types. In a footnote near the end of his essay, Hayek leads us to believe that, despite his references to Popper and to falsification, he in fact has the "common sense" procedure in mind.[44]

The thrust of Hayek's essay is, however, unaffected by the specific type of empirical evidence it recommends. It claims that even pure economics, insofar as it concerns *market* phenomena and not merely the actions of isolated

---

[41] Compare Mises, *The Ultimate Foundation of Economic Science*, pp. 44ff., and *Human Action*, pp. 38-41.

[42] Hayek, "Economics and Knowledge," p. 33; emphasis added.

[43] Ibid., p. 55.

[44] Ibid., p. 47 fn.

individuals, must be partly an empirical or psychological science rather than a logical-deductive one. It must investigate the meanings attached by individual actors to their situation, and it must examine the particular motivations and stimuli that give rise to their choices. It must become a science, not just of action, but of people's *reactions*, and of how these reactions may reflect the use and dissemination of knowledge. Only in this way can economics solve the riddle as to why acting people "should be right."[45] And until it solves this riddle, it cannot say anything certain about market processes.

To put the challenge differently, economic science must establish and examine the mechanisms of *social causation*. It must show that actors in the social world may become reasonably informed of the valuations of other individuals so that they may direct their actions well enough to achieve desired results. Unless this is possible, the formal conclusions of economics, and of praxeology in particular, remain purely hypothetical.[46]

It shall be argued, *contra* Hayek, that the "pure logic of choice" has a great deal to say about the prerequisites for successful action—notwithstanding our ignorance as to the mechanisms of social causation. Moreover, although we shall see that the absence of such causation

---

[45] Ibid., p. 34.

[46] This reference to social causation purposefully avoids mention of the element of time. In fact, as will be shown, what social causation actually implies is not merely that people will have the capacity to understand the *past* valuations of other people, but that they will have some insight into the relationship of these valuations to *future* valuations. Only in this way may actors have reason to assume that, given their own actions A, some set of reactions B will follow rather than an entirely random, unpredictable result. The existence of social causation implies that future social events are in some sense molded by the past. An implication is that there will be a degree of qualitative regularity and uniformity in values and institutions.

would have serious implications, it will be argued that Hayek's suggestion that praxeological conclusions need the support of *an explanation* of social causation (that is, of why it should be that people are ever right) is not very good advice after all.

Shackle

While Hayek criticized "formal" theory for disregarding the role of learning, George Shackle chastised it for its neglect of time. It is important to understand that these criticisms are not the same, although the latter may be considered an extension of the implications of the former. Hayek's critique was largely concerned with the diffusion by the market of knowledge regarding the effects of *past* actions, i.e., its ability to reveal the impact and success of entrepreneurship. Shackle's criticism is much more radical. He concerns himself specifically with the inability of the market to harness and disperse knowledge about the *future*. Thus, he focuses on the failure of formal theory to address the problem of expectations. Moreover, while Hayek suggested the need for economics to explain the possibility of successful (or what we shall later call "coordinating") market actions, he never doubted that the prevalence of such successful action was a *fact*. Shackle, in contrast, has taken just the opposite view.

It is necessary to distinguish two parts of Shackle's critique. First, in what shall be referred to as his "weak thesis," Shackle claims that economic theory neglects the existence of uncertainty. Second, in his "strong thesis," he argues that economic theory cannot deal with the implications of a "kaleidic" future. Only the strong thesis represents a potential criticism of praxeology. It is this thesis that, one may infer, Ludwig M. Lachmann (whose views will be discussed shortly) draws upon in citing the need for praxeology to account for the problem of "divergent expectations."

In expounding his weak thesis Shackle erects a dichotomy that entirely overlooks the praxeological approach. To Shackle, who implicitly equates "formal" theory with neoclassical theory, the only conceivable basis for pure theory is one that identifies rational action with action that is "fully informed."[47] Thus formal theory and its body of deduced relationships are relevant, as he sees it, only to the general equilibrium schema which necessarily excludes the passage of time. Shackle therefore presents the following dilemma: "If there is fundamental conflict between the appeal to rationality and the consideration of the consequences of time as it imprisons us in actuality, the theoretician is confronted with a stark choice. He can reject rationality or time."[48] Clearly, this distressing choice results from Shackle's identification of "rationality" with its neoclassical interpretation according to which rational action is action that *achieves* results more or less identical to those prescribed by the allegedly objective conditions of general equilibrium. Praxeology is entirely unaccounted for in this view of things, for it is at once "formal," giving laws and theorems valid with logical necessity, yet fully applicable to a world of time and its corollary, uncertainty. Indeed, it is only in a world of time and uncertainty that action, the starting point of praxeological analysis, would be possible at all. In a world of perfect certainty and knowledge, individual

---

[47]G. L. S. Shackle, *Epistemics and Economics* (Cambridge, England: Cambridge University Press, 1972), p. 91.

[48]Ibid., in the preface. Cf. also "Time, Nature, and Decision," in *The Nature of Economic Thought* (Cambridge, England: Cambridge University Press, 1972), pp. 71-84.

"actions" would be entirely predetermined. They would be automatic, not purposeful.

Praxeology does not postulate any rigid determinism insofar as *concrete* acts of choice are concerned. The soundness of its deductions is not demonstrated by appeal to forecasting power or its counterpart, empirical falsifiability. Purposeful action involves an ever-present *logical* pattern which praxeology seeks to discover through deduction while avoiding the suggestion that future concrete choices and events in any *scientific* sense be knowable and predictable.

Shackle, on the other hand, cannot conceive of a "pure logic of choice," i.e., of praxeology. He equates formal with "static," unanticipated change with "irrationality." His weak thesis entirely misses the mark insofar as praxeology is concerned. Shackle does not distinguish between neoclassical value theory (based upon the assumption of perfect knowledge and the analysis of a fully determined general equilibrium system of means and ends) and praxeology (which is based upon an analysis of the implications of *action* and necessarily presumes the existence of uncertainty respecting means and ends). Praxeology does not make use of the neoclassical construct that Shackle calls "the rational ideal." Its fundamental basis is a different idea of rationality. According the Mises, this "fundamental thesis of rationalism" is not only consistent with reality but "unassailable":

> Man is a rational being; that is, his actions are guided by reason. The proposition: Man acts, is tantamount to the proposition: Man is eager to substitute a state of affairs that suits him better for a state of affairs that suits him less. In order to achieve this, he must employ suitable means. It is reason that enables him to find out

what is suitable means for attaining his chosen end and what is not.[49]

There is no presumption of perfect knowledge in this doctrine whatsoever. It does not require us to assume that people are infallible. Whether they are or not is a historical problem, not a praxeological one.

Despite these considerations, some Austrian economists are inclined to believe that the criticisms of Shackle's weak thesis apply to praxeology and not just to neoclassical general equilibrium economics. Thus, Lachmann has accused Mises of omitting uncertainty and expectations from his analytical framework.[50] And other Austrians have adopted the practice of referring to praxeology as "static subjectivism," contrasting it with "dynamic subjectivism." Such terminology blurs the distinction between praxeology (which concerns itself with the analysis of action) and conventional neoclassical analysis (which concentrates on the mathematical description of the conditions for general equilibrium or nonaction).[51] Praxeology recognizes that means and ends

---

[49]Mises, *Theory and History*, p. 269. Spiro J. Latsis, in his paper "A Research Program in Economics" (*Method and Appraisal in Economics* [Cambridge, England: Cambridge University Press, 1976], pp. 1-41) is also unable to comprehend the difference between the rationalism of praxeology and that of neoclassical equilibrium analysis. Thus, he describes Mises's principle as one that asserts that "human actions *are adequate or appropriate to the situations in which they occur*" (p. 4, emphasis in the original). In fact, praxeology does not reckon actions as "adequate" or "appropriate." According to it, the actions of a tribal witch doctor are no less rational than those of a modern surgeon. They are simply guided by different beliefs. Thus, contrary to Latsis's suggestion (p. 7), it is impossible for an agent to act in such a way as to "falsify" the praxeological thesis of rationalism.

[50]Kirzner, "Mises and the Extension of Subjectivism," p. 37.

[51]Of course, discussions of evolutionary processes and other exercises in conjectural history may be viewed as more "dynamic" than investigations in the pure logic of choice, but the latter remain dynamic nonetheless.

are not "given" but are rather objects of continuous, subjective reinterpretation. Within such a framework hypothetical constructs based upon the presupposition of perfect knowledge and certainty have only limited value.[52]

Now let us pass briefly to Shackle's strong thesis: the matter of the kaleidic future. Here what may be claimed against praxeology is not that it fails to recognize the categories of uncertainty, time, and expectations, but rather that it fails to reckon with some of the more crucial implications of these. What praxeology fails to account for (insofar as Shackle's strong thesis is concerned)—and what thereby renders its inferences contingent rather than necessary—is how actors may effectively anticipate the future and, in particular, how they may anticipate future actions of other people, given that the future is "unknowable." If people cannot foretell the future, then even the broader, praxeological idea of "rationalism" (which assumes *some*—more than incidental—capacity for actors in the social world to select means appropriate to their chosen ends) is unfounded. Economics is obliged, in this case, not merely to account for the use and dissemination of existing knowledge (as Hayek would have it), but to explain the possibility of entrepreneurial *prediction*.

Lachmann

A still greater challenge to praxeology is present in the writings of Ludwig Lachmann.[53] Lachmann combines

---

[52]Further discussion of the differences between praxeology and neoclassical general equilibrium analysis appears later in this monograph.

[53]See in particular Ludwig M. Lachmann, "Reflections on Hayekian Capital Theory" (unpubl. ms., 1975); "From Mises to Shackle: An Essay in Austrian Economics and the Kaleidic Society," *Journal of Economic Literature* 14 (March 1976): 54-62; and "Mises and the Extension of Subjectivism," in Kirzner, *Method, Process, and Austrian Economics*.

the observations of both Hayek and Shackle to demonstrate what he regards as serious defects in Mises's method.

Lachmann accepts Hayek's description of praxeology as essentially formal and tautological, requiring for its fruitful application to catallactics supplementary hypotheses regarding the use and dissemination of knowledge. Thus, he views Hayek's 1937 essay as "an attempt to set Mises straight."[54] Nevertheless, Lachmann does not entertain empiricist views regarding the need for falsifiable conclusions. Instead, he adopts an unambiguously Schutzian, ideal-type approach, and stresses the need for the economic theorist to build his analysis upon assumptions as to the *typical* thought patterns and choices of acting people.[55] Thus for Lachmann, too, economic theory cannot refer merely to *homo agens* and the incontestable fact of purposefulness. Instead, it must abandon its claims to universal validity and become a branch of history and applied sociology much as Weber had understood it. The pure logic of choice is supplemented by *verstehen* or "common sense" as a theoretical method, which is to serve in the identification of the means by which agents in the real world adapt their actions to match the ever-shifting preferences of their fellows.

Lachmann's most significant innovation, however, is his broadening of Hayek's thesis to allow for consideration of the implications of Shackle's kaleidic future. Alfred Schutz maintained that people could successfully employ understanding ("common sense") in anticipating the future actions of their fellows. While both Mises and

---

[54]Ludwig M. Lachmann, classroom communication.

[55]This point is also stressed in White, *Methodology of the Austrian School*, pp. 26-27.

Hayek implicitly endorsed this conclusion, Shackle refused to acknowledge a "common sense" solution to the problem of choice under uncertainty.[56] Purposefulness, in Shackle's view, is a chimerical notion: Choice is an entirely haphazard process and, therefore (contrary to the praxeological view), it merely appears or is presumed to be rational. Lachmann's embrace of the doctrine that the future is kaleidic thus leads him to doubt the value of praxeology, dependent as it supposedly is upon the assumption that the market harbors a "tendency toward equilibrium."

The particular problem Lachmann emphasizes is that of "divergent expectations." Hayek had stressed the importance of knowledge dissemination in expediting the market process, pointing out the need for market participants to be able to *learn* about the preferences of their fellow human beings and to adjust their actions accordingly. Knowledge dissemination in this context might refer simply to the existence of market signals of profit and loss, the "criteria of success" by which the market judges attempts of agents to understand each other's wants. The problem of "divergent expectations" is more fundamental, for even if the market involves an adequate means for the dispersion of knowledge regarding the appropriateness of *past* actions, the learning involved is not a substitute for, and is in fact useless without, knowledge of the *future*: the "guidance" provided by profit and loss signals is cold comfort in a society marked by kaleidoscopic change. In short, there does not exist in the market any known "criterion of success" that can inform entrepreneurs *ex ante* of the future composi-

---

[56]See Roger Koppl, "Alfred Schutz and George Shackle: Two Views of Choice" (unpubl. ms., 1982).

tion of consumer demands, i.e., of the composition of *plans* and *expectations*. Praxeological conclusions, it follows, are therefore applicable not to acting man or even to perceiving man but only to anticipating man, *homo divinans*. The first task of economics, then, must be to show that real people are of this species. Otherwise, its theories are of doubtful value.

Equilibration and Coordination

Central to the current controversy in Austrian economics is the debate concerning whether or not the market harbors a tendency toward equilibrium. The skeptical position, represented by Lachmann, is that no such tendency exists. It is opposed in particular by Kirzner, who attempts to defend the more traditional, praxeological position.

In this section, an attempt is made to show that there is a strictly logical sense in which action may be said to be equilibrating (rather than disequilibrating), which may be interpreted as implying a tendency toward equilibrium in markets with freely adjusting prices. However, the view defended here contrasts sharply with those of both Kirzner and Lachmann, who are criticized for adopting an analytical framework that is not consistently subjective. The praxeological notion of *equilibration* defended here is also distinguished from the empirical or "common-sense" notion of *coordination* suggested by Hayek, according to which the relevant "tendency" for theorists to be concerned with is one in which the "expectations of the people and particularly of the entrepreneurs will become more and more correct."[57]

---

[57]Hayek, "Economics and Knowledge," p. 45.

To give equilibration a praxeological status is one thing; to show that it is a notion useful in drawing conclusions concerning the efficacy of particular economic arrangements and policies is another. The latter task is undertaken in the second part of the section. The conclusion reached is that, with reference to the purely logical concept of equilibration, it is possible to derive many fundamental results concerning conditions that promote successful action of the sort that Hayek had been so anxious to uncover.

Equilibration

In an autarkic economy composed of a single individual, or in any isolated exchange, all action is equilibrating in the *ex ante* sense; that is, it is expected by the actors involved to lead to the removal of felt uneasiness. In this context, "disequilibrating" action (again viewed in the *ex ante* sense) is impossible; it is the logical equivalent of "irrational" action. For the solitary individual, a tendency toward equilibrium means a tendency for action to systematically eliminate perceived sources of uneasiness. The continuing existence of action is proof that equilibrium proper is never achieved. It is equally proof that it is constantly being striven for. In the case of voluntary exchange between two individuals, equilibrium proper may be said to exist when there is no longer any basis for mutual *profit* (from the point of view of the actors) so that exchange ceases. This "final state of rest," to use Mises's terminology, is the relevant notion of equilibrium in the context of binary exchange. Equilibration in this context means a process by which opportunities for mutual profit are eliminated.

Things are more complicated in the marketplace where there are numerous individuals and indirect exchange. Here, the question of equilibration must address the influence of individual actions upon those not directly involved. In this case, a "tendency toward equilibrium" must be defined in terms of the categories of *entrepreneurial* profit and loss. The tendency is one in which entrepreneurial profits and losses are made to systematically disappear.

The praxeological notion of equilibration applied in catallactics can be summarized as follows: entrepreneurial profit and loss are subjective phenomena, having no "objective" basis outside of the minds of market participants. The praxeologist cannot, therefore, conceive of these phenomena apart from actions of market participants that at once imply imagination of and response to the phenomena in question. Thus for every profit "opportunity," there corresponds an action that eliminates the opportunity (or proves that it was illusory).

Even where there is monetary calculation, only the event of an entrepreneur taking action allows us to distinguish (praxeologically) profits from compensation for opportunity costs and from the pervasive phenomenon of rent. It is necessary, therefore, for praxeology, when dealing with the unhampered market, to treat entrepreneurial profit opportunities as the unique products of the subjective valuations and understanding (*verstehen*) of actors who will seek their exploitation. Upon the fact of action, these "imagined" or "understood" (rather than "perceived") profits are, logically and temporally, destroyed. Thus action leads to the systematic elimination of entrepreneurial profit and loss; it is *equilibrating*. Wherever there is action, there is an imagined profit opportunity. Where there is no action, there are no such imagined opportunities; and where there are no imagined profits, there is no action—that is, viewing things in a dynamic context, there is no basis for the modification of plans.

It must be stressed that equilibration makes no reference to the state of knowledge of market participants. The fact that new information constantly provokes imagination or acknowledgment of new profits and losses (and, hence, their renewed elimination) is recognized by praxeology. Nevertheless, this fact does not contradict the fact of equilibration: it only means that equilibration never ceases and is never replaced by a state of equilibrium proper. This is not to say that questions of knowledge acquisition are unimportant; only pure theory does not address these problems, which have to do with the question of *coordination*. So far, we have not claimed that equilibrating actions generally lead to *desired* or *anticipated* results.

In discussing market phenomena, praxeology does not group commodities according to any "objective" or technological qualities. When it speaks of apparently identical goods bearing different prices, it assigns the discrepancy to a difference in services offered by the goods or by circumstances of their sale or else it must refer to entrepreneurial actions that, in an unhampered market, eliminate the discrepancy. In other words, praxeology recognizes price discrepancies among *identical* goods only to the extent that such discrepancies may be identified with subsequent acts of successful arbitrage. In the same manner, entrepreneurial profit opportunities in general are ephemeral phenomena, formed in the imaginations of enterprising people and *defined* by the very actions that "eliminate" them.

It follows that praxeology must refrain from grouping the services of enterprising people according to "objective" standards, referring to earnings differentials as entrepreneurial profit. It instead assigns these differentials to the category "rent to labor services." Such rent may be said to include an element of profit only insofar as it actually gives rise to imitation by other individuals or to replication by the entrepreneur in question. As each such process of "profit seeking" ceases, remaining money surpluses (differences between money outlays and money receipts) are once again to be viewed as rent or other elements of compensation for opportunity cost. If, however, actors subjectively see in this surplus an element of profit or loss (by way of their imagination or understanding and the use of monetary calculation), they act again to replicate the profit or to eliminate the loss; if they do not so act, it means that neither profit opportunities nor available losses are understood to exist. Every entrepreneurial action therefore begins with the subjective imagination of a profit opportunity (or belief that a loss may be avoided) and ends with the destruction of the imagined opportunity. This, to repeat, is what praxeology means when it asserts that all action is "equilibrating," i.e., that action leads to the systematic elimination of profit and loss.

According to praxeology, competition involves the identification of what had previously been regarded as service rent as "profit" and the resulting efforts to replicate the profit. If, following a series of competitive processes, monetary surpluses still accrue, a renewed sequence of entrepreneurial acts may or may not follow. The important fact is that these surpluses are subjectively (and hence praxeologically) identified with "service rents" or "costs" except when action redefines some portion of them as entrepreneurial profit and thereby proceeds to replicate (and, thus, to eliminate) that profit. It is a mistake to confuse profit with monetary surplus and to describe competition and the tendency towards equilibrium in terms of the "whittling away" of the surplus. This procedure depends upon an objective definition of entrepreneurial profit; it looks upon it as an ideal-type or empirical category to be identified historically by appeal to psychological understanding. In doing so, it confuses the "common sense" point of view adopted by historians and by entrepreneurs themselves with that view of things that is essential to the drawing of conclusions regarding the *necessary* implications or "pure logic" of action. So far as praxeology is concerned, if markets are unhampered (for example, by "rent-seeking" activities), there can be no "unexploited" profit opportunities or lacunae in the competitive process.

Kirzner, Lachmann, and the "Tendency toward Equilibrium"

Entrepreneurs succeed or fail in generating monetary surpluses to the extent that they succeed or fail in anticipating consumer actions. These actions are not predetermined by an unchanging set of preferences. According to praxeology, preferences do not exist at all apart from acts of choice. It follows that all entrepreneurial action is, as this article has insisted, not merely speculative, but *imaginative.* This is true even for "mere" arbitrage (meaning arbitrage as understood by the business community).[58] There is no listable set of profit opportunities (the basis for additions to monetary surpluses) existing independent of entrepreneurial ac-

---

[58]It is therefore necessary to reject Lawrence H. White's attempt to distinguish between arbitrage and entrepreneurship by suggesting that in the former, profit opportunities may be said to have an "objective" existence. See White's essay "Entrepreneurship, Imagination, and the Question of Equilibrium" (unpubl. ms., 1976), p. 4.

tions because there are no consumer preferences apart from consumer actions taken in response to entrepreneurial offers. Thus it is misleading to treat profit opportunities as having an objective basis (i.e., as existing "out there") because it is improper to treat consumer preferences as if they existed apart from realized acts of choice.

Israel M. Kirzner, in his analysis of entrepreneurship,[59] suggests the possibility, in the unhampered market, that action may fail to eliminate entrepreneurial profit and loss systematically, i.e., may fail to equilibrate. This impression results from Kirzner's use of the metaphorical, "common sense" notion of profit opportunities existing "out there" in some objective sense independent of their perception or discovery by enterprising individuals. Kirzner's approach has encouraged the treatment of equilibration as an empirical matter subject to doubt. It is necessary to challenge such interpretations insofar as they confuse necessary features of action with contingent ones and imply that action in the unhampered market may be "disequilibrating" or "insufficiently equilibrating" and that praxeological theorems that presume a "tendency toward equilibrium" are necessarily open to empirical falsification.

The category of objective profit opportunities is praxeologically meaningful only as an *ex post* concept, in which case there is no question of undiscovered opportunities.[60] Yet, the contrary is implied within the frame-

---

[59]Israel M. Kirzner, *Competition and Entrepreneurship* (Chicago: University of Chicago Press, 1973).

[60]While profit opportunities cannot be defined *ex ante* by "objective" criteria (being fundamentally products of entrepreneurial imagination), this does not mean that their successful exploitation *ex post* does not ultimately rest upon appeal to consumer wants. The *success* of entrepreneurial imagination depends crucially upon existence of market prices,

work of Professor Kirzner, who is led to adopt the metaphorical notion of "objective" profit opportunities existing *ex ante* (and hence capable of going undiscovered) in order to counter the opinion that entrepreneurial innovation is disequilibrating. By treating profit opportunities as existing "out there" and by positing their eventual "discovery," Kirzner is able simply to dismiss the innovative (and allegedly disequilibrative) aspects of entrepreneurship.[61] In doing so, he is drawn uncomfortably close to the Robbinsian outlook according to which entrepreneurship merely involves the "efficient" administration of *given* means and ends, that is, the exploitation of given profit opportunities.

In fact it is unhelpful to view, as general equilibrium theorists do, the direction in which market processes are aimed as one that can be represented by a stable system of simultaneous equations. This view entirely neglects human imagination and innovation. It refers to a world where the *means* and *goals* of acting people are fixed, so that a hypothetical "optimal solution" can be defined. This kind of equilibrium solution presupposes definite limits to entrepreneurial achievement. Nonetheless, Kirzner apparently accepts the static concepts of Pareto optimality and general equilibrium as standards against which entrepreneurial actions must be judged. It is only in such a context of "existing" or "given" opportunities that profitable actions can be relegated to the category of "arbitrage," while actions *not* undertaken can be related to "missed" profit opportunities.

---

which inform entrepreneurial understanding. More will be said about this in later sections.

[61]Lawrence H. White, "Uncertainty and Entrepreneurial Expectations in Economic Theory" (unpubl. ms., 1977), pp. 68-69.

More fundamentally, whenever one speaks of unexploited opportunities for profit one departs from the domain of theoretical science and exemplifies the perspective of the historian or would-be entrepreneur. Kirzner's "profit opportunities" exist in the mind of the analyst but are somehow divorced from "the already constituted meanings of active participants in the social world."[62] In other words, the ends-means framework recognized by the analyst differs from that recognized by market participants. The procedure of injecting an independent "imagination" into one's analytical framework takes its revenge by begging important questions, (1) Why should equilibration be a feature of the real world (where actors may be chronically "unalert")? (2) Do praxeological theories that presume equilibration in fact depend upon the soundness of certain empirical assumptions?[63] In contrast, the praxeological approach does away with the question of "alertness" as it disallows the category of "unexploited profit opportunities."

Subjectively defined, equilibration refers to the systematic exploitation of profit opportunities *as they exist in the understanding of market participants*. It makes no reference to any set of "objective" opportunities as determined by the conjectures of the social scientist. Either the set of opportunities is delimited in this strict, praxeological manner, or it is not scientifically delimitable at all.

---

[62]Schutz, *Phenomenology of the Social World*, p. 9.

[63]Thus, even Kirzner is forced to hedge on such fundamental issues as the "completeness" of the competitive process by remarking (in *Competition and Entrepreneurship*, p. 97) that competition is "at least potentially present" even if entrepreneurs fail to be alert.

The claim that all action is equilibrating does not imply that actors are ever actually in a state of equilibrium proper. The concepts "equilibrium" and "disequilibrium" have for the praxeologist a purely heuristic significance. Theorists wishing to explain a process of market price adjustment require a framework upon which to hang the components of their analysis. Thus they adopt a terminological expedient: they refer to the outmoded price, a price that has become incompatible with changes in the apprehended ends-means framework, as a "disequilibrium" price. The appropriate price, that which ineluctably replaces the disequilibrium price as a consequence of actions manifesting the revised understanding of means and ends, is labelled the "disequilibrium" price. The process of price adjustment can only be comprehended by viewing it as a dynamic process of prices which are at once equilibrium prices in relation to those that they have replaced and disequilibrium prices in relation to those that will follow. Because individuals' understanding of ends and means are in constant flux, prices undergo constant revision. But their adjustment is always in the direction of, and never away from, equilibrium, so long as it reflects free entrepreneurial acts. As each price adjustment is itself a vehicle of information about means and ends, it follows that the adjustment of one price may lead to the obsolescence of others. The statement that action is "equilibrating" merely refers to the logical proposition that action continuously accounts for changes in the imagined framework of means and ends, i.e., changes in the structure of imagined profit opportunities.

Ludwig M. Lachmann, who questions the claim that the market harbors a tendency toward equilibrium, takes a view just opposite of Kirzner's by embracing the

Schumpeterian argument that entrepreneurial action is mainly disequilibrating. However, like Kirzner, Lachmann attempts to address the issue of equilibration by employing Walrasian (or Robbinsian) criteria. Equilibrium is viewed by him, not as the focal point of a heuristic lens through which all action can be analyzed, but as a determinate state of affairs defined with respect to some objectively given set of exploitable means and ends. Of course, with respect to such a static ideal, many actions (and innovative actions especially) are disequilibrating. They confound achievement of the equilibrium "solution" by altering the set of "existing" means and ends. People's imaginations equip them to extend the boundaries of the possible. Given that this is so, the idea of equilibration or of a tendency toward equilibrium ought to refer, not to a tendency to approach some *given*, concrete state, but to the tendency of plans to be modified in a systematic way according to the changing imagination, aspirations, and capacities of market participants. Praxeologically, one can abstract from such ever-present change, thereby forcing the means-ends framework to stand still. However, by doing so, one does not succeed in identifying the prerequisites for the achievement of general equilibrium. On the contrary, one *defines* a state of nonaction wherein equilibrium in one sense is already achieved, but, in another, equally meaningful sense is forever out of reach. In other words, the only *meaningful* sense in which action can be said to be equilibrating is the dynamic one which assumes continually changing means and ends and the *absence* of equilibrium proper. In contrast to this subjective, praxeological view, Lachmann's position, like Kirzner's to which he is in part responding, is distinctly nonsubjective: entrepreneurship can only be disequilibrating in the main with respect to a nonsubjective, Walrasian, or static vision of some general equilibrium "target."

The praxeological view just presented attempts, where those of Kirzner and Lachmann have failed, to make sense out of the idea of a tendency toward equilibrium while totally rejecting Walrasian criteria and their implications. By adopting a strictly subjective approach, praxeology also immunizes itself from Lachmann's skepticism (insofar as the *logical* validity of its inferences is concerned—the empirical question of coordination must be addressed later on), preserving the apodictic status of its conclusions which rest upon the premise that entrepreneurial action is equilibrating.

To summarize, "general equilibrium" is a moving target. Its location is determined, not by any objective conditions, but by the confines of people's imaginations. In order for the target to be reached, people either must become perfectly dull or they must become perfectly content. In either case, it must be true that they have exhausted their abilities to conceive of new means for the elimination of uneasiness (the general end of all action). So long as people are neither completely dull nor completely content, they must necessarily act. To ask whether general equilibrium can ever be achieved is therefore to ponder the exhaustibility of people's imaginations. It is to wonder whether innovation and unexpected change will disappear. This is an area of inquiry that concerns philosophy of mind and not praxeology, which is concerned with action. All that can be said with certainty is that people, in acting, employ imagined means to their fullest extent (action is *equilibrating*) and that, if their actions are successful, their imagination and understanding are not based upon illusion and result in increased well-being (action is socially *coordinating*).

Denial of the existence of coordination is in fact the more important part of the current assault upon the praxeological method. We are now prepared to consider this empirical issue. Only first it is necessary to respond to the charge that the praxeological concept of equilibration is "tautological," "empty," and therefore useless as a means for gaining practical knowledge about the real world.

Prerequisites for Successful Action

The concepts of monetary surplus and loss are based on economic calculation using market prices. Such calculation is possible only in an order characterized by exchange, the social division of labor, and private ownership of the means of production. With the aid of monetary calculation, entrepreneurial profit and loss—the stimuli that determine the direction of equilibrative adjustments—become *social* phenomena distinct from the *ex post* categories of psychic profit and loss. Calculation makes possible a link between equilibrating action and entrepreneurs' satisfaction of the wants of others. It allows entrepreneurs to perceive the wants of others as if they were the *means* toward fulfillment of their own *ends*.

Monetary surplus represents a reward to enterprise for the successful satisfaction of consumers. But this *ex post* surplus is not itself to be confused with the *ex ante* concept of entrepreneurial profit: it is a confirmation of the fact that entrepreneurs' imagination and understanding (of means and ends, *including* their own, possibly unique, capabilities) were not based upon illusion or incorrect anticipation of the future. Entrepreneurial profits exist, as it were, only at the "margin" of action, not before or after.

The crucial point is that monetary calculation provides essential guidance for entrepreneurial understanding and action. In the absence of such calculation, the imagination of profit opportunities, i.e., entrepreneurial speculation, would indeed become an entirely haphazard process, bearing no meaningful relationship to the state of consumer preferences: "Monetary calculation is the guiding star of action. . . . [Man] calculates in order to distinguish the remunerative lines of production from the unprofitable ones, those of which the sovereign consumers are likely to approve from those of which they are likely to disapprove."[64]

Without monetary calculation, entrepreneurs would lose vital evidence with which to form their conjectures and would not even be able to judge whether their *previous* conjectures were accurate or not. They therefore would be without means for informed direction of their future actions. It is only when market prices exist that calculation, the meaningful ascertainment of profit or loss, success or failure, is possible. In particular, the entrepreneurial function of subjectively distinguishing "profit" from rents and other factor returns is not conceivable without market prices: "The different sources of income can be separated only be referring to these incomes *as determined by prices on the market*."[65]

Only in this way can an entrepreneur estimate implicit (opportunity) costs and thereby determine that, for example, "he is suffering a loss in his business." Then, "If the loss continues . . . he will be impelled to shift his

---

[64]Mises, *Human Action*, p. 229.

[65]Murray N. Rothbard, *Man, Economy, and State: A Treatise on Economic Principles* (Princeton, N.J.: D. Van Nostrand, 1962), p. 542; emphasis in the original.

various resources to other lines of production. It is only by means of such estimates that an owner of more than one type of factor . . . can determine his gains or losses in any situation and then allocate his resources to strive for the greatest gains."[66]

The existence of market prices, which itself depends upon private ownership and exchange of the means of production, is therefore a necessary prerequisite to economic calculation.[67] This is the fundamental conclusion of the praxeological critique of socialism. The necessity (*not* sufficiency) of market prices for entrepreneurial success, including entrepreneurial calculation and understanding, can be ascertained without appeal to other, necessary assumptions regarding the use and dissemination of knowledge. Its truth does not depend on the "alertness" of entrepreneurs in the unhampered market. It derives from consideration of the pure logic of the equilibration process: in the context of market prices, this process *might* promote coordination. Otherwise, an essential ingredient is lacking, for which there are no promising substitutes.

Many other important, practical conclusions of praxeology are based upon the insight that interference with market prices may disrupt enterprise and competition. Such interference acts to lessen the potential for successful entrepreneurial adjustments in the affected markets. Every act of free exchange provides clues to the preferences and, indirectly, the ends, of actors engaged in the exchange. Market prices convey information reflecting understanding derived through a continuing process of

---

[66]Ibid., p. 543.

[67]Yet these conditions are not sufficient. Successful calculation also depends on entrepreneurial understanding.

such exchanges. Such prices are essential instruments by which entrepreneurs, employing *verstehen* or common sense, attempt to form judgments of consumer desires using past preferences as evidence.

By the same token, interference with market prices may also corrupt entrepreneurial understanding, causing the disappointment of expectations and fostering discoordination. Any nonmarket price—a price fixed by fiat rather than through voluntary exchange—confronts numerous entrepreneurs, not with potentially useful information, but with a lie; it presents to them a façade of preferences and priorities which in fact have no basis in the valuations of market participants. Consumer uneasiness may even be aggravated by entrepreneurial actions guided by nonmarket prices. Hence, the praxeological concern with this type of government intervention.

Praxeology does not attribute the failure of socialism to its inability to achieve the conditions of static equilibrium: on the contrary, socialism cannot succeed, according to praxeology, because entrepreneurial *action* (which includes also the speculative decisions of central planners) cannot succeed without the aid of market prices. Moreover, praxeology sees interference with or absence of competitive market prices as a key to explanation of the failure of many *particular* market processes.[68] For example, the trade cycle is explained as a phenomena initiated by disruption of rates of interest from their "natural" levels, i.e., the levels that reflect consumer time-preference and that would prevail under a system where banks (including central banks) functioned purely

---

[68]Attempts to explain market phenomena by referring to "divergent expectations" or other uncaused "natural" failures of entrepreneurial understanding are not truly explanations at all.

as intermediaries of voluntary savings. An artificially lowered rate of interest and accompanying expansion of credit necessarily leads to the distortion of a wide range of other market prices (by provoking overestimation of the real supply of loanable funds). The *necessary* consequences that arise from this include widespread alteration of profit and loss signals and a greater channeling of entrepreneurial activity into undertakings that eventually prove unsustainable.[69]

In its references to the effects of intervention, praxeology naturally engages in conjectural history. Nevertheless, whenever the described intervention is present,

---

[69]In his article, "The Role of Expectations in Economics as a Social Science" (*Economica* 14 [February 1943]: 108-19) reprinted in *Capital, Expectations, and the Market Process* (Kansas City, Kans.: Sheed Andrews and McMeel, 1977), pp. 65-80, Lachmann denies that the conclusions drawn by the Austrian theory of the trade cycle follow necessarily from the premises involved in that theory. Lachmann claims that a timely adjustment of entrepreneurial expectations may prevent the usual consequences from arising due to the existence of a market rate of interest (r) below the natural rate (n). Mises, in his reply ("'Elastic Expectations' and the Austrian Theory of the Trade Cycle," *Economica* n.s. 10 [August 1943]: 251-52) concedes the validity of Lachmann's claim. Nevertheless, properly worded, the theory remains logically valid; its conclusions refer to consequences that arise *if* authorities succeed in promoting investment beyond levels warranted by the supply of voluntary savings (S_v) by way of the issue of created credit (S_c). Now the market rate of interest, r, is the rate that equates the total demand for bank credit, D, with its *total* supply, $S_v + S_c$, so that the market clears. In the absence of created credit, the market rate r equates S_v with D and so is equal to the natural rate, n. The adjustment of expectations described by Professor Lachmann can only refer to a reduction in D such as is needed to prevent it from exceeding S_v even in the face of the banks' offer of credit at cheaper prices. In other words, the banks' attempt to issue created credit are frustrated. (Alternatively, expectations may operate through the anticipatory raising of prices, so that although the nominal demand for credit rises, there is no increase in real demand.) In either case, the effect is to prevent a divergence between r and n from ever occurring. Therefore, the "elasticity of expectations," far from suggesting a possibility wherein a discrepancy between r and n does not have trade-cycle implications, merely suggests that entrepreneurs may frustrate attempts by banks to create the necessary discrepancy in the first place. The validity of the trade-cycle theory is not affected.

all of the consequences that praxeology attributes to it will follow. It is the task of history proper to determine whether any actual event corresponds to a certain hypothetical counterpart examined by praxeology. This matter of historical identification is, *contra* Hayek, the only "question of fact" to which praxeological conclusions, including ones that (as we have seen) are relevant to catallactics, need to defer.[70] There is no question here of any need for or possibility of "verification" or "falsification" of praxeological theories either in the manner suggested by positivists or by appeal to common sense.

We have still to deal with the implication, present for instance in Hayek's essay, that the results of praxeology, although varied and profound, are nevertheless "tautological" and, therefore, of no independent, practical significance. Here it may simply be answered that if, in fact, praxeological results are tautologies, then they are tautologies of great importance. In a sense, they resemble tautologous statements of the sort: $2 + 2 \neq 5$. This statement, one might claim, provides no fresh knowledge of the real world. Nevertheless, it is essential to insist upon its truth whenever anyone is bold enough to deny it. Similarly, the conclusions of praxeology would perhaps be of little value were there not people anxious to defy them, for example, by seeking to avoid the harmful consequences of inflation by means of price controls, by throwing obstacles in the way of rivalrous competition and entrepreneurial innovation, or by advocating social-

---

[70]This is not to deny that certain propositions generally granted praxeological status may be seen at some point to depend upon unacknowledged empirical assumptions. Yet it is not the case that the greater part of catallactics is comprised of such propositions merely because they presume a "tendency toward equilibrium." This conclusion is defended in the final section of this article.

ism as a means for the rational allocation of resources. The demonstration of the inappropriateness of such programs is the prime contribution of (praxeological) economic theory to human welfare. It is a contribution of more than merely verbal significance.

Thus far, we have seen that many praxeological conclusions (relevant to catallactics) *do not* depend upon assumptions about knowledge, alertness, and entrepreneurial understanding; they deal with people *as such* and do not require appeal to common sense or empirical assumptions. We have also seen that, although logically necessary, conclusions derived by praxeology are not intrinsically empty or without practical importance. However, a complete answer respecting this last point cannot be given until the issue of *coordination* is addressed. We have not yet entirely escaped the claim that praxeology may, after all, be useless.

The "Common Sense" of Coordination

As used in this article, *coordination* and *equilibration* are not synonyms. Coordination, which depends upon the correctness of entrepreneurial expectations, is not a praxeological concept. While we cannot think of free action as nonequilibrating, we can conceive of actions that are noncoordinating. In order to establish whether a particular concrete state of affairs exemplifies coordination or the compatibility of plans, social scientists must resort to the common-sense method of specific understanding employed in historical analysis. They must therefore abandon the strict subjectivism or praxeology and allow themselves to impute specific ends and aspirations to individuals. Then, in order to determine whether the actions of individuals are compatible with one another, they contrast them with an ideal-type "plan" of their own construction. In other words, they treat the actions of other individuals as means and judge their efficacy with regard to a set of imputed ends.

To maintain that individual plans can be coordinated is to affirm the existence of social causation. The idea that such causation operates is related to the belief that social actions are or may be largely *successful*.[71] Praxeology conceives of a sequence of social events as coordinated insofar as they result mainly in psychic profit rather than psychic loss. The notion of coordination thus becomes a corollary to the praxeological construct of the progressing economy.[72]

But to say that progress actually exists requires an appeal to *understanding*: "Whenever economic history ventures to classify economic evolution within a certain period according to the scheme stationary, progressing, or retrogressing, it resorts in fact to historical understanding [*verstehen*] and does not 'measure.'"[73] There can thus be no question of an answer to the question of coordination in any sense admitting to either "apodictic certainty" or to empirical "falsifiability": psychic profit and loss are subjective, immeasurable phenomena.

A progressing economy requires, first of all, that entrepreneurs are neither so dull nor so content as to never imagine opportunities for profit at all. Otherwise, there would be no innovation or accumulation, and society would settle into the praxeological fiction of the "evenly rotating economy." In such a situation, coordination is complete in the sense that there is equilibrium,

---

[71]See Mises, *Human Action*, pp. 22-27.

[72]An exception is the evenly rotating economy, which is a limiting case, as will be discussed later in this article.

[73]Mises, *Human Action*, p. 251.

but it is obviously not coordination in the sense of compatibility of plans, for the evenly rotating economy presupposes the absence of true plans aimed at the elimination of felt uneasiness. It involves, in place of changing plans, the cyclical mechanical motions of lifeless automatons.

Ignoring the extreme case of the evenly rotating economy, coordination requires also that there be adequate entrepreneurial *foresight*; an ability to anticipate future change and to thereby avoid psychic disappointment. Here is where expectations enter into the analysis. It is also where the doctrines of Shackle and Lachmann assert themselves concerning the kaleidic character of the future.

In a world in which the future is truly kaleidic, coordination and its counterpart, economic progress, are not possible. Action in such a world, even in the unhampered market, leads not to "spontaneous order," but to chaos. Speculation becomes a matter of sheer guesswork, useless and counterproductive—and this will be the case even where there is a freely functioning price system. Under such conditions, action cannot truly be said to be "purposeful" at all, for the actors' belief that they are able to achieve their purposes can only be an illusion. Praxeology would in this case be a body of tautologous assertions of academic interest only.

Thus, for example, although the existence of market prices is *necessary* for coordination because it provides the only reliable means for people's actions to be guided by the wants of others, it may not be *sufficient*. It could be that anticipations are generally disappointed, so that wealth does not accumulate. Coordination and its representative, economic progress, will then be impossible even with an unhampered price system.[74] Such possibilities form the crux of the Shackleian challenge to praxeology.

On the face of things, it is easy to sympathize with Kirzner's desire to dismiss the divergent expectations or kaleidic future hypothesis. "Paris," Kirzner observes, "gets fed." This seems to be an appropriate empirical answer to what is in essence an empirical assertion. It might easily be supplemented by a litany of trite observations regarding the accumulation of capital, general improvement of well-being, remarkable scientific and technical achievements, etc., that have been sponsored by the capitalist system. Such a response is also inviting because it suggests that praxeology is not, after all, at loggerheads with historical understanding; that, in general, markets *do* generate order whereas interference tends to have the destructive effects that praxeology predicts. Nevertheless, the response, based as it is upon appeal to common sense, is always vulnerable to rejection. Those who understand by "order" and "progress" something other than what Kirzner has in mind when he refers to the arrival of food at Paris may freely disagree with him. In so doing, they do not, of course, deny the praxeological notion of equilibration. They merely claim that this notion—and the central role it assigns to the existence of market prices—evade the fundamental issues.

In short, praxeology, having broken away from the "fully informed" schema of neoclassical economics, finds its conclusions challenged by alternative views of pre-

---

[74]Lachmann is led to note, concerning the importance of market prices ("Reflections on Hayekian Capital Theory," p. 129), that "The beacon that had been designed to keep entrepreneurs from straying from the narrow path of convergent expectations turns out, on most nights, to be rather dim." It might be countered that a dim beacon is better than none at all, but this answer will not persuade those who believe that the future is truly kaleidic.

cisely the opposite extreme. Its new opponents claim the future to be marked by complete ("radical") uncertainty; a kaleidic future in which action is futile and purposefulness is merely an illusion.[75] If, in fact, this view of reality is correct, then the theories of praxeology are, to repeat Hayek's words, merely "formal" and "tautological." They cannot then tell us anything of practical value, for they are based upon inferences drawn from a faulty premise, namely that qualitative regularity and causality exist in the sequence of social events. The truth, it is suggested, is just the opposite: the future is unknowable; there is no link between it and the past. Expectations are bound, as often as not, to "diverge" and, therefore, to be disappointed. Choice—whether informed by market price signals or not—can only be haphazard under these conditions. Action may make life more and more chaotic. It generates, at best, merely a stationary economy—one with efforts at improvement continually frustrated—and certainly not a progressing economy. It would be just as well if people did not act (i.e., adjust their plans) at all.

Implications of the "Kaleidic Society"

Exponents of the doctrine of the kaleidic society have suggested that the praxeological method presupposes a

---

[75]It is respecting the extremes of perfect knowledge (neoclassical schema) and complete uncertainty ("kaleidic society") that Roger Garrison upholds the view of "Austrian Economics as Middle Ground" (in Kirzner, *Method, Process, and Austrian Economics* (pp. 131-38). Garrison notes that these polar views "represent the extreme circumstances under which economic theory is either trivial or impossible. It is on that expansive band between the two poles that Mises' concept of human action . . . has applicability." See also Oskar Morgenstern, "Perfect Foresight and Economic Equilibrium," in *Selected Economic Writings of Oskar Morgenstern*, Andrew Schotter, ed. (New York: New York University Press, 1976), pp. 169-83.

thesis of historical determinism. They believe that in implicitly rejecting their view, praxeology assumes a rigid link between the patterns of people's actions in the present and their patterns in the future. Such an assumption contradicts the Austrian notion of purposefulness and involves as well a tacit denial of free will.

This representation of praxeology is based upon a serious confusion of its tenets with those of general equilibrium analysis. Moreover, it reveals a failure to appreciate the distinction, recognized by praxeology, between "fatalist" determinism and "activist" determinism.[76] The doctrine of fatalist determinism maintains that the course of social events is beyond human control; its thesis, to the extent that it is accepted, "paralyzes the will and engenders passivity and lethargy among human species."[77] There is no place in this doctrine for purposeful action.

Activist determinism refers to "the insight that every change is the result of a cause and that there is a regularity in the concatenation of cause and effect."[78] It is distinct from fatalist determinism and (therefore from materialism and from what Karl Popper refers to as the "nightmare" of physical determinism[79]) because it allows for the category of *mental* (or social) causation. People's actions, according to the thesis of activist determinism, are "determined" by the ideas (ends, knowledge, and understanding) they hold. But praxeology treats these ideas as ultimate data; it does not seek to explain them

---

[76]On this distinction, see Mises, *Theory and History*, pp. 117-80.
[77]Ibid., p. 178.
[78]Ibid., p. 177.
[79]Karl Popper, "Of Clocks and Clouds," in *Objective Knowledge* (Oxford, England: Oxford University Press, 1972), p. 217.

by tracing them back to prior causes. This is how praxeology separates itself from psychology.

What the current critics of praxeology assert is this: If there is *no* regularity or uniformity in human ideas, if the future is marked by kaleidic change, then people cannot anticipate the actions and requirements of their fellows. Speculation therefore becomes haphazard. Action within society, since it necessarily involves speculation about other people's reactions, although it is believed to be purposeful, is vain. Even routine actions presuppose routine behavior on the part of others. All life in society is thus a random, irrational struggle.

This thesis amounts to a denial of mental or social causation or of activist determinism. Praxeology cannot "prove" this denial to be unfounded. It treats the existence of causality, including social causality, as an ultimate given, a priori even of human purposefulness:

> The philosophical, epistemological, and metaphysical problems of causality and of imperfect induction are beyond the scope of praxeology. We must simply establish the fact that in order to act, man must know the causal relationship between events, processes, or states of affairs. And only so far as he knows this relationship, can his action attain the ends sought. We are fully aware that in asserting this we are moving in a circle. For the evidence that we have correctly perceived a causal relation is provided only by the fact that action guided by this knowledge results in the expected outcome.[80]

The questions of coordination and the possibility of progress are one and the same, both have to do with the existence of social causation. The doctrine that the future

---

[80]Mises, *Human Action*, p. 23. See also, Mises, *The Ultimate Foundation of Economic Science*, p. 20: "All we can say about causality is that it is a priori not only of human thought but also of human action."

is kaleidic, if it means anything at all, means the denial of spontaneous order, coordination, progress, and, fundamentally, social causation, for the first of these are merely manifestations of the last.

No evidence can dispose of the suggestion that the future is kaleidic and that social causation is lacking. Yet current efforts of Austrian economists include attempts to develop a theory of entrepreneurial prediction or understanding that might resolve the problems implied by the uncertainty of the future. This seems to be part of the intent of Rizzo and O'Driscoll in their book *The Economics of Time and Ignorance*.[81] Such work may uncover useful evidence concerning conditions that encourage entrepreneurial success. Nevertheless, it is not likely to satisfy critics who maintain that the future is beyond the grasp of entrepreneurial ability. Any efforts of this new Austrian "research program" to reconstruct praxeology on the basis of a theory of knowledge would in this sense be misguided. The problem is that any explanation of entrepreneurial prediction and understanding must make reference to ideal-type representations of human thought patterns and preferences (as are employed, for example, in Schutz's work). Such representations already *presuppose* the regularity and uniformity rejected by those who hold the future to be kaleidic:

> If an ideal type refers to people, it implies that in some respect these men are valuing and acting in a uniform or similar way. When it refers to institutions, it implies that these institutions are products of uniform or similar ways of valuing and acting or that they influence valuing and acting in a uniform or similar manner.[82]

[81] Gerald P. O'Driscoll and Mario Rizzo, *The Economics of Time and Ignorance* (New York: Basil Blackwell, 1984).

[82] Mises, *Theory and History*, p. 316.

Those who consistently believe Shackle's doctrines are bound to view explanations of human understanding that employ ideal-type constructs as unjustified and question-begging.

The only other recourse open to those who seek an empirical or falsifiable refutation of Shackle's thesis is to attempt an explanation of social causation itself; that is, an explanation of how a person's actions may bring about a particular set of responses on the part of other people. To pursue such a course of study would require one to entertain a belief in strict behaviorism. Attempts to develop a theory of social causation would degenerate into a search for social "responses" to entrepreneurial "stimuli." Were such attempts able to succeed, they could at best provide a basis for a theory, not of people's actions, but of their *reactions*, and would, therefore, encompass a denial of purposefulness. Any such research program must ultimately collapse under the weight of its own self-contradictory presuppositions.[83] But to the extent that it is seriously undertaken by Austrian economists, it would as thoroughly undermine their school's viewpoints as would wholesale adoption of Shackle's views.

Although evidence cannot refute the hypothesis that the future is kaleidic, reason can expose the contradictions that must result from its consistent embrace. Praxeology has employed this approach in the past in criticizing the doctrines of historicism and logical positivism.

The idea that social change is kaleidic implies, as has

---

[83]See Morris Cohen, *Reason and Nature: An Essay on the Meaning of Scientific Method* (New York: Dover, 1978), pp. 334-41.

been shown, the denial of both fatalist and activist determinism. This leaves only the alternative of complete indeterminism: the social events of the future have no necessary connection with those of the past. In such a world, people would have no reason to act. They would have no reason to believe that any particular action (insofar as its success depends upon the valuations of other people) would lead to any particular, desired state of affairs. They could therefore have no basis for preferring one set of actions to another. Such a situation would constitute no less a "nightmare" than Popper's physical determinism. It would, as its proponents suggest, demolish the categories of "order" and "coordination"; but it would also render meaningless the idea of free will. Human will, in order to be useful, must be able to gain some degree of command over its circumstances.

Consistently applied, the doctrine of the kaleidic society must also lead to the abandonment of all quests for knowledge about human action. In the world that it postulates, both theory and history would be useless. People could learn nothing from the past. Moreover, its meaningful investigation would be impossible:

> If that which is becoming were altogether independent of the past and in no way related to it not only would historic events have no connection with each other but we should not have any extended events at all. We cannot speak of any historic process unless there is continuity, unless there are elements of identity between the present and the past.[84]

---

[84]Morris Cohen, *The Meaning of Human History*, 2nd ed. (La Salle, Ill.: Open Court, 1961), pp. 63-64.

Moreover, "to deny that the past molds the future is to deny that there is any continuity or any process."[85] Thus, the search for theory, i.e., for necessary and universal patterns in human action, would be fruitless.

Oskar Morgenstern also has argued that the assumption of radical uncertainty is incompatible with the pursuit of theoretical knowledge:

> Next to the assumption of complete, unlimited foresight, there must be rejected, too . . . the assumption that there exists no foresight at all. That would mean complete [chaos] in the conduct of men. . . . Such an assumption would make the existence of the economy just as impossible as that of economic theory which, as does all science, has to posit a minimum of uniformity in the world. That there is no kind of foresight would be the equivalent to the assertion that acts of the individuals could not be arranged at all. . . . So it can be maintained that some positive degree of "knowledge" as the future behavior, that is, one with more or less established assumptions about the future, is absolutely necessary for the economy.[86]

All theory presupposes the existence of a degree of qualitative regularity and uniformity in the concrete phenomena of reality. The classification of events and institutions presupposes such a belief; so, indeed, does the very existence and use of language. Thus, it is utterly contradictory for upholders of the doctrine that the future is kaleidic to involve themselves in theoretical discussions, especially when such discussions refer to institutions such as banks or money or to classes of events such as the trade cycle or inflation. Such catego-

---

[85]Ibid., p. 64. This is what is implied by the denial of what I have called social causation.

[86]Oskar Morgenstern, "Perfect Foresight and Economic Equilibrium," p. 175.

ries, including all ideal-typical constructs employed in economic history and in the hypotheses of social science, have meaning only by virtue of an appeal to the regularity and continuity of events in the social world. Thus, it is futile to attempt, *pace* Hayek, to explain "why [people] should ever be right." Rather, acceptance of the fact that people can be right is a requirement imposed by the rules of reason themselves. Given this a priori fact, we may proceed directly to consider "why people commit mistakes" without troubling ourselves with attempts to investigate the actual mechanisms of social causation.

Of course, in making these points, I do not pretend to refute the position of an extreme nihilist who would completely deny a place for causality in the sequence of social events. I merely observe that, to be consistent, such a person would have to refrain from making assertions regarding the value and significance of particular market arrangements. More fundamentally, people who wish to deny that there is causation in the social world need to explain their *own* participation in the market and in the discussions of economic theory.[87]

The logical alternative for believers in kaleidic change who seek to engage in economics is to adopt a tempered version of the kaleidic society thesis. In this case, they might maintain that the future is only *poten-*

---

[87] All discourse, scientific or otherwise, presupposes mental causation: it involves belief that there is an exploitable relationship between our ideas and actions and the ideas and actions forthcoming in our fellows. Through discussion, and theoretical discussion especially, one attempts to *cause* others to *change* their beliefs and actions in some anticipatable manner. This is not simply a metaphorical way of putting things. It appears so only because we are thoroughly ignorant of the causal process involved. Similarly, entrepreneurial actions presuppose social causation. This is the basis for the belief on the part of entrepreneurs that they may successfully predict (understand) and influence the future choices of others.

tially kaleidic and that history does witness temporary periods of relative stability and even progress. In the midst of such intervals, institutions exist that possess a degree of permanence. Economic theory may deal with these institutions and with the human actions that give rise to them, although it must recognize that its conclusions are never a description of necessary or universally valid truths. This outlook, of course, defines historicism. There is no point in repeating here the familiar epistemological arguments that oppose it.[88]

To summarize: Praxeology cannot refute historicism or any other variant of the thesis that the future is unconnected with the past. It treats the category of causality, including mental and social causality, as a priori. It assumes a world marked neither by perfect certainty nor by kaleidic change and continually diverging expectations. In other words, it takes as given a set of conditions that make *purposeful* human action possible, and it then asks what circumstances hamper, and which ones assist, the likelihood of agents' success. In proceeding in this manner (instead of seeking to actually explain "why men should ever be right"), praxeology takes the only route available to theory that avoids self-contradiction. It adopts as its starting point—but does not try to explain—"the actual persistence of human habits and institutions" that "is one of the great facts of history which we cannot ignore if we are to retain any understanding."[89]

A stalwart might still argue that praxeology, like Euclidian geometry, is purely formal and arbitrary

---

[88]Cf. Mises, *Epistemological Problems*, chap. 2, and Carl Menger, *Problems of Economics and Sociology* (Urbana: University of Illinois Press, 1963).

[89]Cohen, *Human History*, p. 64.

rather than necessarily true. On this view, praxeology may not apply to any actual experience of social reality. But expressing the argument in this manner immediately reveals its absurdity, for to imagine a social "experience" to which the logic of action does not apply is to imagine away social experience altogether. This is because the idea of "experience" itself presupposes the categories of causality and regularity on which praxeology depends: "In a universe lacking [regularity] there could not be any thinking and nothing could be experienced. For experience is the awareness of identity in what is perceived; it is the first step toward a classification of events. And the concept of classes would be empty and useless if there were no regularity."[90]

So long as there can be meaningful experience of social phenomena, then this experience will be one for which the deductions of praxeology are valid. To imagine otherwise is to imagine a social environment free from meaningful experience altogether. Thinking and acting people cannot consistently regard their world as one in which the laws of praxeology are mere formalities.

Of course, it may be that a world exists in which praxeology would not provide useful knowledge. But this would not be a world in which either purposeful action or economic knowledge mattered or would be possible. The observations of any "nonpraxeological" economics, even if valid, could not serve any useful purpose. Furthermore, theories of "knowledge dissemination" and of the "market process," however informative they may be,

---

[90]Mises, *The Ultimate Foundation of Economic Science*, pp. 15, 21.

can no more "replace" praxeology than they can undermine the doctrine of the (radically) kaleidic society. Nor should they be viewed as prerequisites to the drawing of valid praxeological conclusions.

References

Blanshard, Brand. *Reason and Analysis*. La Salle, Ill.: Open Court, 1973.

Bowley, Marian. *Nassau Senior and Classical Economics*. New York: Octagon Books, 1967.

Cohen, Morris R. *The Meaning of Human History*. 2nd ed. La Salle, Ill.: Open Court, 1961.

———. *Reason and Nature: An Essay on the Meaning of Scientific Method*. New York: Dover, 1978.

Egger, John B. "The Austrian Method." In *New Directions in Austrian Economics*. Edited by Louis M. Spadaro. Kansas City, Kans.: Sheed Andrews and McMeel, 1978, pp. 19-39.

Harris, Errol E. *Hypothesis and Perception: The Roots of Scientific Method*. London: George Allen & Unwin, 1970.

Hayek, Friedrich A. "Economics and Knowledge." In *Individualism and Economic Order*. Chicago: University of Chicago Press, 1948, pp. 33-56.

Kirzner, Israel M. *Competition and Entrepreneurship*. Chicago: University of Chicago Press, 1973.

———. *The Economic Point of View*. Kansas City, Kans.: Sheed and Ward, 1976.

———, ed. *Method, Process, and Austrian Economics: Essays in Honor of Ludwig von Mises*. Lexington, Mass.: Lexington Books, 1982.

Knight, Frank H. "The Limits of Scientific Method in Economics." In *The Ethics of Competition and Other Essays*. New York: Harper Bros., 1935.

Koppl, Roger. "Alfred Schutz and George Shackle: Two Views of Choice." Unpublished ms., Spring 1982.

Lachmann, Ludwig M. "From Mises to Shackle: An Essay on Austrian Economics and the Kaleidic Society." *Journal of Economic Literature* 14 (1) (March 1976): pp. 54-62.

———. *The Legacy of Max Weber*. Berkeley, Calif.: Glendessary Press, 1971.

———. "Reflections on Hayekian Capital Theory." Unpublished ms., 1975.

———. "The Role of Expectations in Economics as a Social Science." In *Capital, Expectations and the Market Process*. Kansas City, Kans.: Sheed Andrews and McMeel, 1977, pp. 65-80.

Latsis, Spiro, J. "A Research Program in Economics." In *Method and Appraisal in Economics*. Cambridge, England: Cambridge University Press, 1976, pp. 1-41.

Menger, Carl. *Problems of Economics and Sociology*. Edited and Translated by James Dingwall and Bert F. Hoselitz. Urbana, Ill.: University of Illinois Press, 1963.

Mill, John Stuart. *Essays on Some Unsettled Questions of Political Economy*. 2nd ed. London: Longmans, Green, Reader, and Dyer, 1874.

Mises, Ludwig von. "'Elastic Expectations' and the Austrian Theory of the Trade Cycle." *Economica* n.s. 10 (August 1943): 251-52.

———. *Epistemological Problems of Economics*. Translated by George Reisman. New York: New York University Press, 1981.

———. *Human Action: A Treatise on Economics*. 3rd ed. Chicago: Henry Regnery, 1966.

———. *Notes and Recollections*. Translated by Hans F. Sennholz. South Holland, Ill.: Libertarian Press, 1978.

———. "Profit and Loss." In *Planning for Freedom*. 2nd. ed. South Holland, Ill.: Libertarian Press, 1962, pp. 108-50.

———. "The Treatment of 'Irrationality' in the Social Sciences." *Philosophy and Phenomenological Research* 4 (4) (June 1944): 527-53.

———. *The Ultimate Foundation of Economic Science*. Kansas City, Kans.: Sheed Andrews and McMeel, 1978.

Montague, William Pepperall. *The Ways of Knowing*. London: George Allen & Unwin, 1925.

Morgenstern, Oskar. "Perfect Foresight and Economic Equilibrium." In *Selected Economic Writings of Oskar Morgenstern*. Edited by Andrew Schotter. New York: New York University Press, 1976, pp. 169-83.

O'Driscoll, Gerald P., Jr., and Mario Rizzo. *The Economics of Time and Ignorance*. New York: Basil Blackwell, 1984.

Popper, Karl. "Of Clocks and Clouds." In *Objective Knowledge: An Evolutionary Approach*. Oxford, England: Oxford University Press, 1972, pp. 206-55.

Rothbard, Murray N. "In Defense of 'Extreme Apriorism.'" *Southern Economic Journal* 23 (3) (January 1957): 314-20.

———. *Man, Economy, and State: A Treatise on Economic Principles*. Princeton, N.J.: D. Van Nostrand, 1962.

———. "Praxeology: The Method of Austrian Economics." In *The Foundations of Modern Austrian Economics*. Edited by Edwin G. Dolan. Kansas City, Kans.: Sheed Andrews and McMeel, 1976, pp. 19-39.

Schutz, Alfred. "Common Sense and the Scientific Interpretation of Human Action." In *Philosophy of the Social Sciences*. Edited by Maurice Natanson. New York: Random House, 1963, pp. 302-46.

———. *The Phenomenology of the Social World*. Translated by George Walsh and Frederick Lehnert. Evanston, Ill.: Northwestern University Press, 1967.

Shackle, G. L. S. *Epistemics and Economics: A Critique of Economic Doctrines*. Cambridge, England: Cambridge University Press, 1972.

———. "Time, Nature, and Decision." In *The Nature of Economic Thought*. Cambridge, England: Cambridge University Press, 1972.

Shils, Edward, and H. L. Finch, eds. *Max Weber on the Methodology of the Social Sciences*. Glencoe, Ill.: Free Press, 1949.

White, Lawrence H. "Entrepreneurship, Imagination, and the Question of Equilibrium." Unpublished ms., 1976.

———. "The Methodology of the Austrian School of Economics." Auburn, Ala.: Ludwig von Mises Institute, 1984.

———. "Uncertainty and Entrepreneurial Expectation in Economic Theory." Unpublished ms., 1977.

About the author ...

George A. Selgin is an assistant professor of economics at the University of Georgia. He received his Ph.D. from New York University in 1986 and was lecturer in economics for a year at the University of Hong Kong. His first book, *The Theory of Free Banking: Money Supply Under Competitive Note Issue* was published in 1988 by Rowman and Littlefield.

About the Ludwig von Mises Institute...

Founded in October 1982, the Ludwig von Mises Institute is a unique educational organization dedicated to the work of Ludwig von Mises and the advancement of Austrian economics. The Institute's board is chaired by Mrs. Ludwig von Mises. The founder and president is Llewellyn H. Rockwell. Professor Murray N. Rothbard, Professor Mises's top American student, is vice president for academic affairs.

In six decades of teaching and writing, Professor Mises rebuilt the science of economics, and the defense of the free market and honest money, on a foundation of individual human action. From then on, Marxists, Socialists, and Keynesians might retain their positions of power in governments and universities, but they had been defeated in the intellectual battle.

Ludwig von Mises dedicated himself to scholarship and freedom. The Mises Institute pursues the same goals through an extensive program of:

- Publications, including the twice-annual *Review of Austrian Economics* edited by Murray N. Rothbard; the monthly *Free Market*; the quarterly *Austrian Economics Newsletter*; books; monographs; and occasional papers in theory and policy.
- Fellowships and assistantships for Misesian graduate students.

- The O. P. Alford, III, Center for Advanced Studies in Austrian Economics.
- Academic centers at Auburn University and the University of Nevada, Las Vegas.
- Teaching programs and seminars, including the annual summer "Mises University" at Stanford.
- Conferences on such subjects as the gold standard, the Federal Reserve, taxes, Marxism, Keynesianism, bureaucracy, socialism, and the work of Ludwig von Mises and Murray N. Rothbard.
- The Henry Hazlitt Fund for Economic Journalism.
- The Lawrence Fertig Student Center.
- Public policy work in Washington, D.C., on the free market and gold standard.

For more information on the Institute's work, please write: the Ludwig von Mises Institute, Auburn University, Auburn, Alabama 36849.